£1·49
W26

KU-175-745

THE COMPLETE JUICER

Text and Photographs by Lionel Martinez

RUNNING PRESS
Philadelphia, Pennsylvania

To Barbara, Joe and Calamity for the usual; Alma and John Kowalski for juicing decades before anyone else; John Phillips for pertinent information; and Georgia Knisley for odds and ends.

Copyright © 1992 by Running Press
Printed in the United States of America
All rights reserved under the Pan-American and International Copyright Conventions.

This book may not be reproduced in whole or in part in any form or by any means, electronic or mechanical, including photocopying, recording, or by any information retrieval or storage system now known or hereafter invented, without the written permission of the publisher.

Canadian representatives: General Publishing Co., Ltd., 30 Lesmill Road,
    Don Mills, Ontario M3B 2T6.
International representatives: Worldwide Media Services, Inc. 115 East Twenty-third Street,
    New York, New York 10010.

9 8 7 6 5 4 3 2 1

Digit on the right indicates the number of this printing.

Library of Congress Cataloging-in-Publication Number 92-53812

ISBN 1-56138-185-3

Cover design: Toby Schmidt

Designed and produced by AM Publishing Services and Benford Books
    227 Park Avenue
    Hoboken, New Jersey 07030
Editorial and Design Director: Tony Meisel
Editor: Barbara Fultz
Art Director: Cassandra Perkins
Photographer: Lionel Martinez
Glassware: D.F. Sanders & Co., 952 Madison Avenue, New York, New York 10021

This book may be ordered by mail from the publisher.
Please add $2.50 for postage and handling.
But try your bookstore first!
Running Press Publishers
125 South Twenty-second Street
Philadelphia, Pennsylvania 19103

CONTENTS

JUICING FOR HEALTH AND TASTE

Every morning most people begin their day with a glass of juice. For the majority this is the last time they will ever see any juice until the next morning. To those early morning juice drinkers, juice is a commercially-bought item that comes in cans, bottles or cartons. It is not fresh; it is missing nutrients.

Most processed juices boast about their vitamin and mineral content. This is not derived from naturally occuring nutrients, but added later, from vats containing chemical approximations of the major vitamins and minerals found in fresh juices. Many minor and trace elements that are found in fresh natural juices are lost in commercial processing. The addition of gross supplements can make up for these subtle losses. Fresh raw juices contain all these missing nutrients.

We have moved away from our organic roots. Much of our lifestyle is disconnected from the earth. This not a plea for a "back to nature" movement, it is the way things are. Scientists now theorize that the prehistoric human diet derived a major portion of its nutrients from plants. Much of this food was eaten raw, four or five times throughout the day. There is a growing belief that our bodies need this steady intake of nutrients to maintain good health. Juicing raw fruits and vegetables can maintain this flow of nutrition.

Juicing extracts vitamins and minerals in one quick procedure. Unlike eating pounds of bulk which take hours to digest, juices are easily digested, because they are mostly water. They are an efficient way to consume raw plant nutrients.

The joys of juicing are not limited to great nutrition. Wonderful tasting juice combinations can be made with a flick of the switch. Many favorite fruits and vegetables can be combined into glorious non-fattening liquid snacks that will brighten that rainiest day.

Another, less obvious, benefit is the use of the juice extractor in cooking. Until now almost all recipes called for vegetables and fruits to be cooked down to a mush to extract their flavorful liquids. These flavor essences can now be used in their purest form. Like the blender and the food processor, the juice extractor stands proudly in the kitchen, an indispensable aid to preparing any meal.

THE NUTRITIONAL JUICER

Juicing is an efficient and pleasant way to give your body the nourishment it needs. Unlike eating raw fruits and vegetables, a glass of healthful juice quickly puts nutritious vitamins and minerals into your bloodstream without having to wait hours for your stomach to digest the cellulose and fiber. Sometimes the normal digestive process misses and even destroys vital nutrients. Juicing can be seen as a predigestive technique that makes maximum use of available vitamins and minerals found in fruits and vegetables.

Several glasses a day of fresh vegetable and fruit juice mixtures provides another important health benefit often overlooked by most people: a continuous replenishment of nutrients lost in normal daily living. According to the former Surgeon General C. W. Koop, "...adequate nutrient and energy intake is critical to the maintenance of optimum immune function." An adequate intake often means a continuous intake.

What is an adequate intake of vitamins and minerals? Anyone with the slightest interest in his own nutritional health has seen the Federal Drug Administration's charts of required daily allowances of vitamins and minerals. These charts are based upon the minimum amounts of nutrients needed to prevent vitamin deficiency diseases. Best known of these disorders is scurvy. Scurvy was the bane of ocean-going sailors from the fifteenth to nineteenth centuries. The lack of vitamin C caused this degenerative disease. Even before vitamin C was discovered the British learned, early in the nineteenth century, that scurvy could be prevented by including citrus fruits in the sailor's diet. The fruit frequently used by the English were limes, hence the name "Limeys" to signify members of the British navy.

Prevention is an admirable goal, but it does not really address the idea of maximum nutrition. If the recommended daily allowance (RDA) of vitamin and mineral intake is based on preventing disease, what is the optimum daily allowance to insure uninterrupted good health?

An interesting nutritional phenomena is occurring on America's farms. For over twenty years animal breeders have been feeding their livestock vitamins and minerals five to ten times in excess of the animal's RDA. This is done to ensure that the farmer's livestock will survive in a healthy state when the animals are taken to market. In overall terms the herds are remarkably free of disease during their lifetime.

Some medical authorities have attributed this state of well-being to the use of antibiotics in the feed, and not to the use of vitamins. But not all livestock that are fed vitamins are fed antibiotics and they still remain free of disease. Although more research remains to be done in this area, it seems that vitamins are the deciding factor in the livestock's good health.

The vitamins fed to the farm animals are not given in one massive dose, but rather in several large portions at each feeding. The nutrition is spread out during the day, allowing the animals to replenish what each individual needs at the time. What is not needed is eliminated in the urine. Peak levels of nutrition are thus maintained throughout the day.

Sustaining your personal optimum daily allowance of vitamins and minerals may be necessary to prevent sub-clinical vitamin deficiencies. A growing number of nutritionists believe that the predisposition to various diseases begins at the cellular level with a barely adequate intake of vitamins and minerals. At this degree of nutrition vitamin deficiency diseases are absent, but full nutrition has not been attained. The body's cells receive enough nutrients to maintain minimal life functions. They do not receive enough vitamins and minerals to protect themselves from long term wear and tear. Even-

tually the cells die prematurely, the body becomes less resistant to various disorders and some unwanted ailment strikes.

Although this scenario is an over-simplification of complex biochemical processes, it does represent the dangers that some nutritionists believe result from less than optimal nutrition. Sub-clinical deficiencies can be avoided with a continuous supply of vitamins and minerals.

Drinking three to four glasses of fruit and vegetable juices at different times during the day is an excellent way to insure a continuous daily supply of nutrients. In the right combinations it is healthier to have a glass of nutrition-packed juice than to take a vitamin and mineral supplement.

Commercial supplements frequently lack balanced nutrition. In some cases the vitamin pill formula is missing a nutritive helper that enables the body to process important elements. An example would be a vitamin and mineral supplement that contains 10 milligrams of iron, but not enough vitamin C and calcium to aid the body to fully take advantage of the iron. Another problem is that many trace elements and recently discovered nutritive substances are missing from manufactured supplements. Often these nutrients work synergistically with vitamins and minerals by either boosting their value to the body or by aiding in proper metabolism of the substances. Fruits and vegetables often contain many

complementary nutrients that help the body
metabolize the ingested vitamins and minerals.

Juicing is not the answer to all of your
nutritional needs, it is a valuable addition to
your effort to maintain good health.

PEAR JUICE

FRUITS AND VEGETABLES

Following are the most common fruits and vegetables used in juicing with their respective uses, nutritional information and notes on preparation and health.

APPLES

NUTRITIONAL DATA: Apples are a very good source of vitamin C. Vitamin A is present only when the skin is juiced along with the fruit. Vitamins B-1, B-2, B-6, folic and pantothenic acid are also found in lesser amounts. Potassium heads the list of minerals found in apples; found in lesser amounts are copper, magnesium and phosphorus.

USES: The vitamin and mineral content of apple juice helps to maintain the immune system against colds and the flu. The minerals are especially good in promoting healthy skin and hair. Pectin is found in large amounts in apple juice. This substance is the same as found in over-the-counter commercial antidiarrheal medicines. High in natural sugars, apples make good juice sweeteners.

NOTES: When using apples in a juice recipe be careful to wash any wax from the skin. Be sure to remove the seeds before you juice. Apple seeds contain a naturally occurring cyanide/sugar compound that will deteriorate into hydrogen cyanide over time. A few seeds won't hurt you, but five or six apples' worth might make you ill. Because of apple juice's high pectin content it interferes with the body's absorption of dietary fats. Those people who have problems in digesting fats should should limit the amount of apple juice in their recipes.

ASPARAGUS

NUTRITIONAL DATA: The slender stalks of the asparagus pack a wallop of nutrition. Not only does asparagus contain large amounts vitamins A, C, K and the B complex, but asparagus is also a good source of plant protein. Rounding out the nutritional package are the minerals iron and potassium.

USES: Asparagus juice can be used as a mild diuretic. It is safe when used in moderation. This slender plant also contains the amino acid asparagine. Asparagine is believed by some nutritionists to aid in the removal of wastes from soft tissue. This cleansing effect makes asparagus juice a perfect way regain one's balance after a binge of rich over-cooked foods.

NOTES: Vitamin K facilitates the normal clotting of human blood. Foods rich in vitamin K, like asparagus, may offset the effectiveness of anticoagulants. People taking drugs to dissolve clots and thin the blood should consult their doctors before using vitamin K rich vegetables in their juicing recipes.

BEAN SPROUTS

NUTRITIONAL DATA: Bean sprouts contain vitamin A and the B complex of vitamins, but the B complex is less than what is found in fully mature beans. On the other hand, bean sprouts have four times the amount of vitamin A than beans. These stringy bean wannabes have a fair amount of protein and are rich in iron and potassium.

USES: Use bean sprouts as an easy mixer for most vegetable juices. They are also good in any recipe that is rich in iron, since the high vitamin C content aids in iron absorption.

BEETS

NUTRITIONAL DATA: There are an abundance of natural sugars and complex carbohydrates in beets. The real nutritive benefit from beets comes from their mineral and trace element content. Beets contain choline, iron, potassium and manganese as well as the amino acids: lysine, phenylalanine and valine. Beets also contain moderate of amounts of vitamins C and A.

USES: The amino acids and trace elements in beets makes their juice a powerful blood and kidney cleanser. When mixed with high energy juices, beet juice can provide that fresh, ready-to-go feeling before strenuous sports activities.

NOTES: Although beet juice is known for its kidney cleansing properties, it should be avoided by anyone on a strict diet to control kidney stones. Raw beets contain oxalates that can bind with calcium and can form kidney stones.

BROCCOLI

NUTRITIONAL DATA: Broccoli has as much vitamin C as fresh orange juice and as much calcium than as milk. This sustaining plant is also high in vitamins A, E and K as well as such minerals as selenium and potassium. Forty five percent of the calories in broccoli are made up of protein. But in order to utilize this protein broccoli juice must be mixed with another high protein source. See NOTES.

USES: If you wish to enhance your immune system you could not find a better juice. Broccoli juice will work well in protecting the gastrointestinal and respiratory tracks from infections.

NOTES: Because the proteins found in broccoli

are incomplete in their amino acid make up, it is best to combine broccoli juice with more complete juice, like bean sprouts. People with thyroid conditions should avoid broccoli since it contains a group of chemicals called goitorgens that may cause enlargement of the thyroid. Healthy people will not have any adverse effect. Anyone taking a test for hidden blood in the stool should not have broccoli juice within 48 hours of the test. It will produce a false positive result.

CABBAGE

NUTRITIONAL DATA: Vitamin A is found in the green patches on the cabbage leaf. The whole vegetable is rich in Vitamin C as well as moderate amounts of vitamin K, calcium, potassium and organic sulphur.
USES: Cabbage juice has a positive effect on the lower intestinal track. This cousin of the Brussel sprout also has a reputation for restoring energy and vitality, especially on the cellular level. The vitamin, mineral and trace element content of cabbage juice helps to maintain the immune system against environmental damage from industrial chemicals and cigarette smoke.
NOTES: Some people produce gas due to a bad reaction to the organic sulphur and liquified food fiber found in cabbage. In most cases just using a small amount of cabbage juice in a recipe will bypass this reaction. People with thyroid conditions should avoid cabbage since it contains a group of chemicals called goitorgens that may cause enlargement of the thyroid. Cabbage contains vitamin K and may offset the effectiveness of anticoagulants.

CARROTS

NUTRITIONAL DATA: Except for red peppers there is not another vegetable with such a high vitamin A content. In addition, carrots contain moderate amounts of the B complex and vitamin C, iodine, manganese, potassium and the amino acids arginine, hisidine, tryptophane, and valine. With such a high vitamin A content, carrots will prevent night-blindness due to vitamin A deficiency.
USES: Some nutritionists believe that drinking carrot juice on a regular basis is an excellent way to remove toxins from the liver. Carrots will also protect the larynx, esophagus and respiratory tract from mnay toxic chemicals in the environment.
NOTES: It is possible to over do a good thing. The pigments found in carrots are fat-soluble. These pigments collect in the fatty tissues just under skin. Drinking large amounts of carrot juice for more than a month will give your skin an odd yellow appearance. Carrot juice will produce a false positive result in the guiac test for hidden blood in the feces. Anyone taking such a test for hidden blood in the stool should

not have carrot juice within 48 hours of the test.

CELERY

NUTRITIONAL DATA: Celery juice contains a moderate supply of vitamins A and C. It is rich in minerals such as calcium, manganese, potassium and organic sodium and sulphur.

USES: Because of celery juice's calcium and organic sulphur content, drinking celery juice is an excellent way to aid digestion and counteract an acid stomach. Some herbalists believe that regular use of celery juice will maintain a healthy complexion. The organic sodium content of this vegetable makes celery juice a perfect mixer and natural way to add zest to your recipes.

NOTES: Use only fresh celery. Moldy or damaged stalks contain certain chemicals which may cause the skin to become painfully sensitive to light on contact.

CHERRIES

NUTRITIONAL DATA: This time consuming juice rewards the user with bountiful amounts of vitamins A, C and a lesser quantity of the B complex. Cherry juice is very rich in potassium and contains a lesser amount of cobalt, magnesium and phosphorus.

About a quarter of a cherry's weight comes from its pit and this pit must be removed before juicing, but it is well worth the effort in terms of flavor and health benefits.

USES: Herbalists use cherry juice to ease the discomfort of joint disorders as well as to reduce blood acidity.

NOTES: Be sure to remove the pit before you juice cherries. The pit contains a naturally occurring cyanide/sugar compound that will deteriorate into hydrogen cyanide over time.

CUCUMBER

NUTRITIONAL DATA: The cucumber is a member in good standing of the squash family. Although cucumbers have small amounts of the B complex and vitamin C they are very rich in minerals like calcium, magnesium, phosphorus and potassium.

USES: Cucumber juice is very, very good for the skin, hair and nails. Some nutritionists have found that drinking cucumber juice and following a moderate regimen of exercise promotes muscle flexibility. There is also a mild natural diuretic action noted with drinking cucumber juice.

NOTES: Try to buy unwaxed cucumbers. If this is not possible, and in all likelihood it is not, peel the skin before juicing. The wax which gives the cucumber its shiny appearance does not wash away with soap.

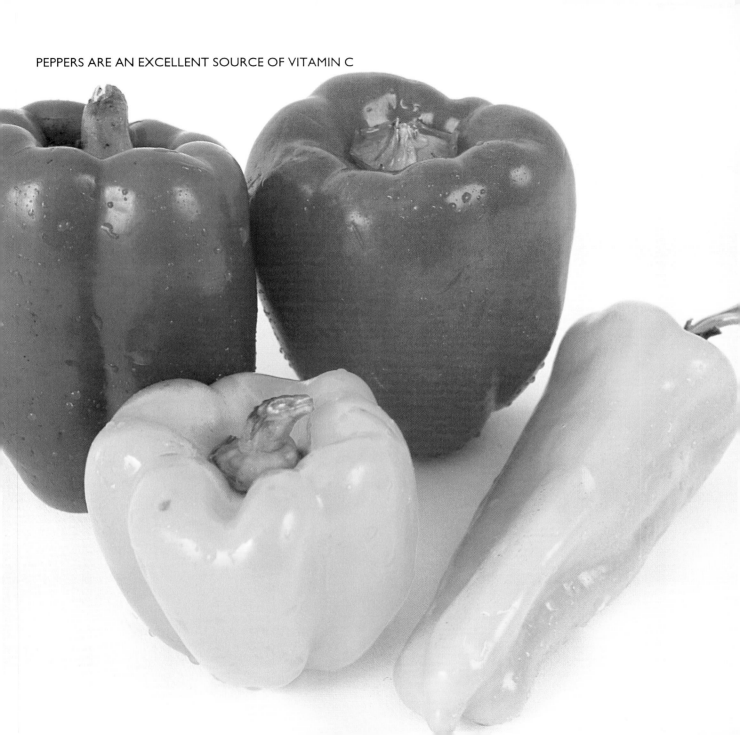

PEPPERS ARE AN EXCELLENT SOURCE OF VITAMIN C

DANDELION GREENS

NUTRITIONAL DATA: Each spring home-owners fight the invasion of the dandelions. What they don't know is that this weedy intruder is also a storehouse of nutrition. Dandelion greens are packed with the B complex, vitamins A and C, plus generous amounts of calcium, iron, magnesium, phosphorus, potassium and trace elements.
USES: Dandelion greens juice has shown some effect in protecting the gastrointestinal and respiratory tracts from infections. There is also reason to believe that dandelion greens juice will offer some protection against toxic chemicals released into the environment. Because of their bitter taste, dandelion greens are best used in combination with other juices.
NOTES: Vitamin K facilitates the normal clotting of human blood. Foods like dandelion greens,that are rich in vitamin K, may offset the effectiveness of anticoagulants. People taking drugs to dissolve clots and thin the blood should consult their doctors before using vitamin K rich vegetables in their juicing recipes. Dandelion greens juice contain oxalates that can bind with calcium and form kidney stones and should be avoided by anyone on a strict diet to avoid kidney stones.

GARLIC

NUTRITIONAL DATA: Garlic is high in vitamins C and B1, as well potassium, iron and selenium. Some of the potent beneficial organic compounds include allyl, disulphide allicin and alliin. This distant relative of the onion packs a culinary and nutritional punch.
USES: The compounds allicin and alliin found in garlic have been shown to have a mild antibiotic effect in laboratory and animal studies. Other studies have shown that garlic also offers some protection against against circulatory diseases. Besides the aforementioned health benefits a small amount of garlic juice will add pep to tired mundane recipes.
NOTES: Not much garlic is needed to gain the feeling of increased vim and vigor in a matter of weeks. The only downside to using garlic on a daily basis is the possibility of garlic breath and body odor. One way to counteract this problem is to add parsley to your garlic recipes.

GRAPEFRUIT

NUTRITIONAL DATA: Like other citrus fruits, grapefruit juice contains a powerhouse of vita-min C. In addition grapefruit juice offers fair amounts of the B complex as well as vitamins E, and K. Potassium is the foremost mineral in grapefruit followed by calcium and potassium.
USES: Daily but moderate intake of fresh citrus

fruit juice will help to prevent colds and aids in strengthening capillary walls and healing wounds. If you drink juices rich in vitamin C along with eating foods rich in iron, the vitamin C will enhance your body's ability to absorb the iron.

NOTES: Because of its high pectin content grapefruit juice interferes with the body's absorption of dietary fats. Those people who have problems in digesting fats should should limit the amount of grapefruit juice in their recipes.

GRAPES

NUTRITIONAL DATA: Grape juice delivers moderate amounts of vitamins A, C and the B complex. Phosphorus is the main mineral found in grape juice and about 8 percent of grape juice's calories is made up of plant protein. In addition to the usual vitamin and mineral content, grape juice is rich in the natural sugars dextrose and fructose.

USES: Many European slimming diets have emphasized the use of fresh grape juice because of its natural sugars. This may seem to be a contradiction, but the theory is that the dextrose and fructose act as appetite suppressors and keep the dieter from feeling hungry during the day. Grape juice also helps to eliminate wastes and toxins from the kidneys.

NOTES: Keep grape juice in non-metal containers to prevent the juice from changing into ghastly shades of blue, purple or yellow. A little lemon or orange juice will pleasingly change red grape juice into a brighter and richer red color. Grape and grape juice fasts are popular in Swiss health spas. Care should taken not to overdue such fasts for more than one or two days without medical supervision.

JERUSALEM ARTICHOKES

NUTRITIONAL DATA: Vitamins A and C as well as the minerals calcium and potassium are found in great abundance in Jerusalem artichokes.

USES: High in natural sugars, Jerusalem artichokes make good juice sweeteners. Jerusalem artichokes are a welcome addition to weight gain juice recipes.

NOTES: Jerusalem Artichokes contain inulin. Some people have confused this complex and inert sugar for enzyme insulin. Inulin does not react with the human body in any way. Insulin is necessary for the sugar metabolism and can only be made by mammals, not plants. This mistake may have been due to a typographical error committed over 40 years ago, but the myth that Jerusalem Artichokes contain insulin has persisted to the present.

KALE

NUTRITIONAL DATA: Vitamin A is found in the green patches on the kale leaf. The whole veg-

etable is rich in vitamin C as well as moderate amounts of vitamin K, the B complex, calcium, potassium and organic sulphur.

USES: The vitamin, mineral and trace element content of kale juice helps to strengthen the immune system against environmental damage from industrial chemicals and cigarette smoke. Kale is one of the high alkalai vegetables, good for restoring alkali-acid balance.

NOTES: Foods like kale, that are rich in vitamin K, may offset the effectiveness of anticoagulants. People taking drugs to dissolve clots and thin the blood should consult their doctors before using vitamin K rich vegetables in their juicing recipes. Kale juice contain a moderate amount of oxalates that can bind with calcium and form kidney stones. Caution in using this juice should be exercised by anyone on a strict diet to control kidney stones.

LEMONS AND LIMES

NUTRITIONAL DATA: Although these citrus fruits taste very different, their nutritional profile is very similar. Both lemon and lime juice have a high vitamin C content which is complemented by a fair amount of bioflavonoids, potassium and calcium.

USES:A little of either one of these fruit juices adds a lot of flavor to most recipes. Both lemon and lime juice have a diuretic effect without harming the kidneys. Lemon juice was used in the nineteenth century as a natural antiseptic. French experiments showed that lemon juice killed many bacteria, including typhoid, in time periods ranging from 20 minutes to 3 hours.

NOTES: Canker sore sufferers may experience a flare up after drinking lemon or lime juice. Avoiding these citrus juices does not prevent such attacks.

LETTUCE

NUTRITIONAL DATA: There are several types of head lettuce. Following is an average nutritional content for iceberg, romaine, Boston and leaf lettuce. In general, lettuce contains moderate to good amounts of vitamins A, K and C. Minerals range from potassium, calcium, iron and traces of iodine. Surprisingly, a moderate amount of protein can be found in most types of lettuce. Romaine lettuce has highest vitamin A content of any lettuce.

USES: Natural tranquilizers are found at the core of most head lettuce. These substances are noted for their calming effect and make good muscle relaxants.

NOTES: There is enough vitamin K in lettuce to warrant caution on the part of anyone taking anticoagulants.

MELONS

NUTRITIONAL DATA: Only the yellow melons,

cantaloupe, Persian and honeydew, include vitamin A in their nutritional profile. All melons have vitamin C as well as a low amount of the B complex and high potassium content. Melon juice is a perfect summer time thirst-quencher and that is good because that's when they are in season.

USES: Some nutritionists have noted a mild diuretic action associated with melon juice.

NOTES: Those people who feel bloated after eating melons following a large meal should drink melon juice on an empty stomach. This mild indigestion may be fermentation caused by the melon juice interacting with the food in the stomach.

ORANGES

NUTRITIONAL DATA: A good deal of the vitamin C found in this citrus fruit is concentrated in the white fibrous layer that rests under the peel. In addition to containing potassium and calcium, oranges are a rich source of bioflavniods.

USES: Orange juice is a must for any tropical recipe. In fact many recipes that call for sugar, like marinades or certain sauces, can be further enhanced by substituting orange juice. In a recent survey orange was found to be America's number one flavor. Laboratory experiments with animals have shown that foods rich in bioflavonoids help to keep capillaries strong and healthy. Oranges,

rich in vitamin C and bioflavonoids, can help speed the healing process in many people.

NOTES: Those people prone to canker sores may experience a flare up after drinking orange juice. Avoiding orange juice does not prevent such attacks.

PAPAYAS

NUTRITIONAL DATA: Papayas are rich in vitamins A and C. They are also loaded with magnesium, phosphorus, potassium and organic sulphur.

This tropical fruit is noted for its papain content. Papain is a natural enzyme that can break down complex proteins into simple molecules. Extracted papain is the main ingredient in meat tenderizers.

USES: Rich in folklore, papaya juice has long been used as an aid in cases of indigestion and flatulence. Papaya pulp moistened with a small amount of juice had been used in the tropics as a beauty treatment to lift dead flaky skin.

NOTES: Test a small area of the skin to see if you have an allergic reaction to papain before you use papaya juice as a beauty treatment. Anyone taking anti-depressants or anti-hypertensives containing an MAO inhibitor must not drink papaya juice under any circumstances.

PARSLEY

NUTRITIONAL DATA: Both an herb and a vegetable, parsley contains a high quantity of vitamins A and C and a lesser quantity of thiamine, riboflavin and niacin. It is rich in such minerals as calcium, magnesium and potassium. Parsley is very rich in chlorophyll, the natural breath freshener.

USES: Parsley can be mixed in juice recipes with such odorous ingredients as garlic and onions to combat offensive breath. There are few vegetables that can match parsley juice's reputation as an overall body cleanser. It has been used in herbal medicine as diuretic, kidney and bladder cleanser and immune system booster.

NOTES: Parsley juice has a very potent effect on the body, a little goes a long way. Juicing parsley concentrates all its nutrients and in liquid form it should not be used for more than three or four days in a row.

PARSNIPS

NUTRITIONAL DATA: This starchy carrot-like root is a good source of vitamin C as well as calcium and potassium. Parsnips have a strong flavor and are best used in combination with other vegetables.

USES: Any recipe with parsnip juice will enhance the nutrition needed for the good health of skin, nails and hair.

NOTES: Only use fresh parsnips. Moldy or damaged roots contain certain chemicals which may cause the skin to become painfully sensitive to light.

PEACHES

NUTRITIONAL DATA: The fuzzy peach contains a good quantity of vitamin A and fair amounts of vitamin C, B1, B2 and niacin. Calcium and potassium round out the peach's mineral content. Peach juice has been noted for its mild laxative effect when taken daily.

USES: Potassium replacement regimens often include peaches.

NOTES: Be sure to remove the pit before you juice. Peach pits contain a naturally occurring cyanide/sugar compound that will deteriorate into hydrogen cyanide over time. A pit won't hurt you, but several might make you ill.

PEARS

NUTRITIONAL DATA: Vitamin C, a small amount of the B complex and a generous potassium content make a pear's major nutritional profile.

USES: There is also a significant amount of fiber which is not lost in the pulp because it resides in the flesh as little gritty particles. Pear juice is very sweet and can be mixed with other fruit juices and diluted with water. The natural fiber found in pear juice makes it a good laxative. It also has a very mild diuretic effect while at the same time replacing the potassium usually lost by taking diuretics.

PINEAPPLES

NUTRITIONAL DATA: The juice of the exotic pineapple contains substantial amounts of potassium, calcium, phosphorus and organic sulphur, as well as moderate amounts of iron, and the vitamins A and C.

USES: Like the papaya, pineapples contain a natural enzyme that can break down complex proteins into simple molecules. It is called bormelain. Pineapple juice has long been used in tropical folk medicine as an all-around aid against indigestion and constipation.

NOTES: Anyone taking a test for serotonin in the urine should avoid pineapple juice for at least three days. Such tests are used to determine the presence of endocrine and gastrointestinal tumors.

PLUMS

NUTRITIONAL DATA: Vitamins A and C are found in great abundance in plum juice. Iron and potassium are found in lesser amounts. In addition to vitamin and mineral content plum juice contains a fair measure of fruit acid salts.

USES: Due to its stimulating effect on the intes-tines, plum juice can be used in cases of consti-pation and hemorrhoids.

NOTES: Be sure to remove the pit before you juice. Plum pits contains a naturally occurring cyanide/sugar compound that will deteriorate into hydrogen cyanide over time.

RADISHES

NUTRITIONAL DATA: Radishes, a distant cousin to the cabbage, have a healthy amount of vitamin C in addition to a moderate quantity of iron and potassium.

USES: Radish juice is usually used in combina-tion with other vegetable juices and taken before meals for its stimulating effect on the appetite. It also has a very strong diuretic action.

NOTES: People with thyroid conditions should avoid radish juice since it contains a group of chemicals called goitorgens that may cause enlargement of the thyroid. Healthy people will not feel any adverse effect. Anyone taking a test for hidden blood in the stool should not have radish juice within 48 hours of the test. It will produce a false positive result.

SCALLIONS

NUTRITIONAL DATA: Of all the onion family, scallions or green onions contain the most vitamin C and A. Scallion juice is a good source of calcium, iron, potassium and organic sulphur.

PINEAPPLE JUICE CAN BE AN AID TO INDIGESTION

USES: Recent laboratory studies discovered that the essential oil found in scallions, and in onions generally, lower levels of LDLs (bad cholesterol) and raise levels of HDLs (good cholesterol). Scallion juice can be used as a diuretic and herbalists in Germany recommend using it as a mild anti-parasite treatment.

NOTES: Although not as strongly flavored as their rounder cousins, scallions can still cause flatulence, halitosis and indigestion in some people. Juice both green and white parts of the scallion, since each part contains a different set of nutrients.

SPINACH

NUTRITIONAL DATA: Spinach is high in vitamin C and it contains a goodly amount of vitamin A and the B complex. There is an ample quantity of phosphorus, potassium, magnesium and trace elements in spinach.

It is also high in calcium, iron and protein. But these nutrients are not easily utilized by the body because the protein is considered incomplete and iron and calcium absorption is minimized by the presence of oxalic acid.

USES: It is best to use spinach juice in combination with other juices, especially if you mix it with vegetables containing protein. Spinach juice stimulates the liver and has a mild laxative effect. People taking drugs to dissolve clots and thin the blood should consult their doctors before using vitamin K rich vegetables like spinach in their juicing recipes.

NOTES: Raw spinach contains oxalates that can bind with calcium and form kidney stones. Those people who have a tendency toward kidney stones should use spinach juice sparingly. Anyone one taking anti-depressants or anti-hypertensives containing an MAO inhibitor must not drink spinach juice under any circumstances.

STRING BEANS

NUTRITIONAL DATA: String bean juice has an ample supply of vitamins A and C that are complemented by iodine, iron and potassium. This is not a stand-alone juice, it has an odd thick texture and must be mixed with other juices.

USES: The main reason to use string bean juice is for its bracing effect on the body's metabolism. String bean juice will also help restore alkali balance.

SWEET PEPPERS

NUTRITIONAL DATA: Sweet peppers contain high concentrations of vitamin C and sweet red peppers have very high concentrations of vitamin A. Both red and green peppers have a good measure of iron and potassium.

USES: Pepper juice is not very appealing alone. It

is very good as a flavor added to vegetable juices. Your hair, nails and skin will appreciate the addition of sweet pepper juice to your favorite juice recipes.

NOTES: Red peppers are actually mature green peppers. Vitamin A undergoes a tenfold increase during this maturation process in sweet peppers.

TOMATOES

NUTRITIONAL DATA: Tomato juice is an important source of vitamin C. There is a real difference between tomatoes grown outdoors and those that are raised in a hothouse. Hothouse tomatoes have half the vitamin C content of outdoor tomatoes. Both hothouse and outdoor tomatoes have the same amount of potassium and calcium.

USES: Eaten as a vegetable, the tomato is really a berry that is a fruit. Tomato juice is a flavorful mixer with strong flavored juices. Fresh juice is not so thick as the canned or bottled varieties and is much less acidic. Some herbalists claim that fresh tomato juice is a wonderful liver cleanser.

NOTES: Under no circumstances should you juice the leaves from vine ripened tomatoes. They contain solanine, a powerful nerve poison. Ingesting these leaves can cause illness and in great quantities, death. It is possible to overdo a good thing. The pigments found in tomatoes are fat-soluble. These pigments collect in the fatty tissues just under skin. Drinking large amounts of tomato juice for more than several weeks will give your skin an odd yellow appearance.

JUICES CAN AID IN CLEANSING THE BODY

JUICE FASTS

As defined in the dictionary fasting is either partial or complete abstinence from food. Other than for religious or political reasons fasts are usually undertaken for health reasons. The health theory behind fasting states that by limiting your intake of food the body gets a chance to eliminate stored-up waste materials at a time when very little new food is being added to the body.

Total fasting has been practiced since ancient times, perhaps even before recorded history. It is a very austere form of fasting. Water is usually the only substance taken into the body. Such fasting done for more than a day puts a strain on the constitution and can do more harm than good. When total fasting is practiced for a few days it can bring on gout and severe depression as well as the loss of lean body tissue. In the elderly, long-term total fasts can precipitate heart rhythm abnormalities.

Going on a juice fast for a day or two can avoid the dangers of total fasting, while giving the body a chance to purge built-up toxins. Juice fasts are not true fasts since nourishment is still being added to the body, albeit at a greatly diminished level.

An extra benefit of any juice fast is weight loss. Since fewer calories are consumed, the body burns fat tissue for its daily quota of energy. But a juice fast should never be used as a quick method to lose weight. Real and permanent weight reduction can only be achieved by a healthy change in eating habits. Juice fasts can help a diet, but you should consult your doctor about a good weight reduction plan.

If you should decide to perform a juice fast you should bear in mind a few helpful pointers:

Juice fasts work best in your free time, not during your regular work schedule. Keep your social and business commitments light. Do not overextend yourself, and relax. Some juice fasters find it helpful if they meditate during the fast. Exercise moderately and try not to push yourself to new limits of physical endurance.

The juice fast is a time to flood your body with fluids. Beginning with your first glass of juice in morning, drink fluids even when you don't feel thirsty. Most juice fast authorities say that you should consume at least three quarts of liquid during each day of the fast. The recommended three quarts of liquid include the 3-6 eight-ounce glasses of juice each day. These other liquids can be in the form of any combination of plain water, herbal teas and lemon water. Lemon water consists of three tablespoons of lemon juice to a cup of water.

The essence of the juice fast is the substitution of 1-2 eight ounce glasses of juice for each of the daily main meals. The morning juices usually consist of fresh fruits, the lunch juices can contain either fruit or vegetable juices and the evening juices are for the most part just vegetable juices.

Breaking the fast is just as important as fasting. Due to the lack of solid intake, the stomach shrinks in size while fasting. When you break your fast you must begin eating small amounts of food more often than usual, about 5 or 6 times a day. The first small meals should be made up of fresh fruits and steamed vegetables. Nothing fancy, just simply cooked meals. For the next few days do not tax your stomach with complex sauces and fatty foods; broiled and steamed cooking is the best bet. Once your stomach has regained its original size, a matter of day or two, you may go back to a normal pre-fast diet.

PLENTY OF PULP

The pulp that is the byproduct of juicing shouldn't be thrown away. In its pulverized state it can be added to a compost heap where—mixed with leaves, grass clippings and other organic matter—it will add fast-decomposing qualities to the mix.

You need fiber for regularity and good health. Pulp can be used to add fiber to sauces, main courses, baked goods and toppings. It works well as a natural and healthful thickener for sauces and stews. And it can add color and body to a wide variety of dishes.

Throughout this book, you will find recipes that utilize pulp in various ways. Try them. You'll be suprised.

HEALTHY DRINKS

Now that you have your juicer, how do you start making healthful drinks? Most beginners start with single vegetable and fruit juices.

The most popular vegetable is the carrot. It produces a milky, orange-colored juice that is like a frothy snack in a glass. A few juicing authorities claim that carrot juice will not keep for any period of time. This is partially true, for the liquid will lose some of its fresh taste several hours after being juiced; but any remaining carrot juice can be used in many cooking recipes, days later, with no discernible loss in carrot taste.

This juicing adventure is eagerly continued with celery, apple, orange and tomato juices copiously flowing from the tireless juicer. Once you have tasted these single juices you'll be ready for some simple combinations.

SIMPLE COMBINATIONS

Again we must return to the carrot because it is used as a base for many juice drinks. By far the favorite carrot juice combination with new and experienced juice makers alike is carrot-orange.

CARROT–ORANGE JUICE

This popular juice is now making its way into the supermarkets as a bottled commercial preparation. It will never match what you can do at home.

2 carrots, washed, lightly scraped and tops removed
2 oranges, peeled and depithed

Cut the carrots and oranges to fit into the juicer feed tube. Juice and enjoy. Makes 1 glass.
For a snappy change of pace juice a half-inch cube of ginger with the carrots and oranges.

Sometimes a vegetable tasting drink is preferable to a sweet drink like carrot-orange.

CARROT–CELERY JUICE

Another popular juice which can settle a slightly upset stomach due to its celery content.

*1 1/2 stalks of celery, washed and the bitter tops
removed*
*3 carrots, washed, lightly scraped and tops
removed*

Slice the carrots and celery to fit into the feed
tube. Juice. Makes 1 glass. Although this is not a
sweet juice, a small cube of ginger would make a
great occasional zesty addition.

CUCUMBER–CELERY JUICE

Cucumbers contain a lot of water and this juice is
not as thick as one containing carrots. Don't let
its thin appearance fool you. This juice is loaded
with vitamins and minerals.

1 cucumber, peeled
*3 celery stalks, washed and the bitter tops
removed*

Put hopper-ized pieces into the juicer and enjoy.
Makes 1 glass.

APPLE–CELERY JUICE

2 apples, seeded and cored
*2 celery stalks, washed and the bitter tops
removed*

APPLE–BLUEBERRY

1 apple, seeded and cored
1 pint blueberries, hulled

CARROT–STRING BEAN

*2 carrots, washed, lightly scraped and tops
removed*
1 cup string beans, washed

APPLE–PEAR

1 apple, seeded and cored
1 pear, seeded and cored

MULTI–INGREDIENT JUICES

Juices with three or more ingredients have their
origins in homeopathic and herbal medicine.
Many of these recipes were or still are believed to
help in building the immune system, cleansing
the body or restoring vitality. The scientific
proof of these claims has been either verified,
disproved or not yet examined.

A case in point is the 1992 discovery of the
chemical sulforaphane found in broccoli, brus-
sels sprouts and other cruciferous vegetables.
This substance was found to stimulate protective
enzymes in human cells that protect against the

ORANGE JUICE MAKES A DELICIOUS JUICE BASE

formation of cancerous tumors. But claims made by some juicing advocates for the wondrous powers of vitamin U are completely out-of-line, since vitamin U does not exist.

There may be other chemicals to be found in fruits and vegetables that will be shown to be very beneficial to human health. In the meantime, while we wait for these substances to be discovered, it doesn't hurt to have several glasses of juice each day; it can even be fun.

THE BIG RED V

Your own homemade version of the commercial vegetable cocktail drink. This is also a great all purpose tonic.

3 tomatoes, washed
2 carrots, washed, lightly scraped and tops removed
3 celery stalks, washed and the bitter tops removed
2 bell peppers, either red or green, seeded
1 cup spinach, washed
1/2 beet, washed
1 clove garlic
1/2 teaspoon lemon juice
salt to taste

Cut all the vegetables into hopper-sized pieces. Bunch up the spinach. Juice. Add the lemon juice and salt. Makes 1 large glass.

SKIN AND HAIR COMBINATION

All these ingredients have been said to have a beneficial effect on both hair and skin.

1 cucumber, peeled
1/2 cup parsley, Italian or flat
3 asparagus stalks, washed
1 cup spinach, washed

Slice the cucumber and asparagus into hopper-sized pieces. Bunch up the spinach. Juice. Makes 1 glass.

THE GREAT COMPLEXION COMBINATION

Not only is this juice a wonderful skin tonic, it tastes good, too. If watercress is not available substitute an equal amount of parsley.

3 carrots washed, lightly scraped and tops removed
1 tomato, washed
1/2 cup watercress
1 cucumber, peeled
1 stalk broccoli, washed, tough bottom stalk removed

Cut all the vegetables into hopper-sized pieces. Bunch up the watercress. Juice. Makes 1 large glass.

IMMUNE SYSTEM SPECIAL I

According to some holistic practitioners this blended juice offers good protection against viral infection.

1 cup blackberries, hulled
1/2-inch cube ginger root, peeled and coarsely chopped
1 cup grapes, red or white, split and seeded
1 carrot, washed, lightly scraped and top removed
1/2 teaspoon lemon juice

Push the blackberries through the hopper, followed by the ginger root, grapes and carrot. Add the lemon juice. Stir until well mixed, and enjoy. Makes one glass.

IMMUNE SYSTEM SPECIAL II

The trace elements found in these vegetables will help to keep your immune system at its best.

3 carrots, washed, lightly scraped and tops removed
2 broccoli stalks, washed, tough bottom stalks removed
2 asparagus stalks, washed
1 red bell pepper, washed and seeded
1 cup parsley, washed
1 clove garlic

Cut all the vegetables into hopper-sized pieces. Bunch up the parsley. Juice all the ingredients. Makes 1 large glass.

VEGETABLE FOUNTAIN OF YOUTH

At present, no juice or miracle substance can make you younger. But you can slow the aging process with a proper diet, exercise and a daily glass of this juice combination. If kale is not available, parsley may be substituted.

1 cup kale, washed
1 cup spinach, washed
2 carrots, washed, lightly scraped and tops removed
1 cucumber, peeled
1 tomato, washed

Bunch up the kale and spinach. Slice the carrots, cucumber, tomato into hopper-sized pieces. Juice. Makes 1 large glass.

FRUIT FOUNTAIN OF YOUTH

A refreshing high energy drink, especially good after an exercise session.

1/2 papaya, seeded
1 cup strawberries
1 cup grapes, red or white, split and seeded
1 orange, peeled and depithed

1 carrot, washed, lightly scraped and top re-
moved
1 1-inch square ginger root, peeled and coarsely
chopped

Scoop out the papaya and juice. Put the strawberries, grapes, orange and carrot into the hopper,
continue juicing. Finish juicing with the ginger
root square. Stir and enjoy. Makes 1 large glass

GREEN CLEANSER

Holistic medicine advocates make a strong case
for the internal body cleansing properties of
many vegetables. Here is a recipe full of these
green cleansers.

1 cup cabbage, chopped
1 cucumber, peeled
1 cup parsley, Italian or flat
3 asparagus spears
1 celery stalk, washed and the bitter tops re-
moved
1 teaspoon lemon juice

Cut all the vegetables into hopper-sized pieces.
Juice. Add the lemon juice and stir. Makes 1
large glass

A LIVER–CLEANSING JUICE

Raw beets have been used traditionally by

herbalists as a liver cleanser. Care should be
taken not to overdo this recipe; do not use it as
part of a daily regimen.

3 beets, washed, tops removed
1 celery stalk, washed and the bitter tops re-
moved
1/2 cup dandelion greens, washed
1 cup watercress

Cut the beets and celery to fit into the hopper.
Bunch up the dandelion greens and watercress.
Juice. Makes 1 glass

MEMORY TONIC

This complex juice can help your memory to be
as sharp as any twenty-year old.

2 stalks broccoli, washed, tough bottom stalks
removed
3 carrots, washed, lightly scraped and tops
removed
2 asparagus stalks
1/2 cup parsley
1 1-inch cube ginger root, peeled and coarsely
chopped
1 tablespoon kelp powder (available at any
health food store)
2 tablespoons almonds, shelled and ground

Cut the vegetables into hopper-sized pieces.

Bunch up the parsley. Juice all the vegetables. Transfer the juice to a blender or food processor. Add the kelp and the ground almonds. Blend until well mixed. Pour into a glass. Makes 1 glass.

SLEEPY—TIME COCKTAIL

Lettuce is a treasured folk tranquilizer and an aid for sleeplessness. Drink this juice a half-hour before bedtime.

3 cups lettuce, any variety, washed
2 stalks celery, washed and the bitter tops removed
1/2 cucumber, peeled

Bunch up the lettuce and juice. Cut the celery and cucumber into hopper-sized pieces and juice. Pour into a glass and stir. Makes 1 large glass.

AFTERNOON LIFT

Replace that afternoon snack with an invigorating, pick-me-up juice.

3 carrots
3 celery stalks
1 tomato
1/2 clove garlic
1 scallion
1 1-inch cube ginger root,
2 tablespoons walnuts, ground

Cut the carrots, celery and tomato into hopper-sized pieces. Juice all the vegetables. Feed the garlic, scallion and ginger root into the hopper and juice. Transfer the juice to a tall glass. Add the walnut powder. Stir. Makes 1 large glass.

FUN DRINKS

FRUIT SHAKES

Fruit shakes sprang into being with the invention and consumer distribution of the blender. This class of liquid refreshment was further elaborated on with the advent of the food processor and juice extractor.

Early shakes tended to consist of whatever fruit was available plus the addition of some thickening agent. Both of these ingredients were plopped into the newly purchased blender and processed until they became an homogenized brew. It was soon realized that it was possible to overdo a good a idea and ten-fruit combinations, tasting like a sweet pulpy mess, were abandoned for more thoughtful mixtures.

Some people call fruit shakes smoothies. The differentiation is in name only, and was anonymously named to put as much distance as possible between the healthy fruit shake and the popular sugar-and-animal-fat-loaded milk shake.

Whether they are called smoothies or fruit shakes these fun drinks share certain common attributes. They are made with fresh fruit and fruit juices. They are thickened with one of the following: yogurt, bananas, milk, ice cream or ice. Extra sweetening is usually added in the form of raw sugar, refined sugar, artificial sweeteners, honey or maple syrup.

Almost any fruit can be used for a fruit shake. If it cannot be juiced, it can be blended into the shake using a blender or food processor. The most common juices for a smoothie are either orange or apple juice. Strawberries, raspberries, blueberries and others are the traditional solid fruits.

Fruit shake purists tend to use yogurt, bananas and ice as thickeners. Milk and ice cream are shunned by the faithful. Those with a more laissez faire attitude will occasionally include those other dairy products in their fruit shakes.

Yogurt produces a thick and tart smoothie. Banana-thickened fruit shakes are heavy and have a sweet tropical taste. When ice is used as a thickener the shake must be consumed before the ice melts. Milk and ice cream will make a shake resemble the diner and luncheonette variety, except that it will contain real fruit.

A BERRY COOLER

Refined sugar should be avoided. Artificial sweeteners are just that—artificial. Raw sugar is okay to use, although it will still create the feeling of a "sugar rush" that one gets from refined sugar. Honey and maple syrup are the most popular fruit shake sweeteners, but each of these organic sugars will give the smoothie a distinctive flavor.

What fruit you use and how you thicken and sweeten your fruit shake is up to you. But there is no reason to reinvent the wheel, so here are some time-tested favorites.

SUNRISE SURPRISE

An energy-packed way to start the day when you don't have time for a full breakfast.

5 strawberries, hulls removed
1/2 cup yogurt
1 cup orange juice
2 tablespoons sweetener (your choice)

Put the strawberries and yogurt in a blender or food processor and blend until well mixed. Add the orange juice and sweetener and process again. Serve. Makes one tall glass.

RASPBERRY DREAM

A good summer sipping drink.

1/2 cup raspberries
1 cup yogurt
1/2 cup pear juice
1 tablespoon sweetener (your choice)

Blend the raspberries and yogurt in a food processor or blender for 15 seconds. Add the pear juice and sweetener and blend again until well mixed. Makes one glass.

BERRY COOLER

If you love berries then this refreshing fruit shake is for you.

6 strawberries, hulled
1/4 cup raspberries
1/4 cup blackberries
1 cup pear juice
1 teaspoon sweetener (your choice)
6 ice cubes, crushed

Put the the berries in a food processor or blender. Process until the berries are puréed. Add the pear juice and sweetener. Blend until the mixture is smooth. Add the ice cubes and give the fruit shake a ten second burst, or until the liquid is smooth. Makes one large glass.

TROPICAL DELIGHT

You don't have to go the Caribbean to have a taste of pristine white beaches on sun drenched islands.

6 strawberries
1/2 mango, peeled and seeded
1 banana
1 1/2 cups orange juice
1 tablespoon sweetener (your choice)
1/2 teaspoon lime juice
1/8 teaspoon fresh mint, chopped

Combine the strawberries, mango, banana and orange juice in a food processor or blender. Process until the mixture is smooth. Add the lime, sweetener and mint and process once more for about five seconds. Makes 2 glasses.

WATERMELON COCKTAIL

This thirst quencher is to be sipped, not gulped.

1 cup watermelon juice
1 cup raspberries, hulled
1/4 teaspoon lime juice
8 ice cubes, coarsely crushed

Combine the watermelon juice, raspberries and lime juice in a blender or food processor. Blend until the mixture is smooth. Add the crushed ice and process for 15 seconds. Makes 1 large glass.

EXOTIC PAPAYA

A gift from romantic places, a fruit shake to be shared by two.

1/2 papaya, peeled and seeded
1 banana
1 cup pineapple juice
1/2 cup orange juice
2 tablespoons lemon juice
1 tablespoon sweetener (your choice)
1/8 teaspoon cinnamon, ground

Put the papaya, banana and pineapple juice into a blender or food processor. Process for 10 seconds. Add the orange juice, lemon juice, sweetener and cinnamon. Blend until the mixture is smooth. Makes 2 glasses.

CANTALOUPE–PEAR NECTAR

Any in-season melon can be substituted in this smoothie.

1 cup cantaloupe cubes
1 cup pear juice
1 tablespoon lime juice
1/2 cup yogurt
1 tablespoon honey
1/8 teaspoon allspice

Combine the cantaloupe cubes, pear juice, lime juice and yogurt in a food processor or blender. Process until the all the ingredients are well mixed. Add the honey and allspice and process once more. Makes 1 tall glass.

HIGH ENERGY TIGER'S MILK

This is not your typical fruit shake. It is a highly nutritious and energizing meal in a glass.

3/4 cup yogurt
3/4 cup orange juice
1 banana
2 strawberries, hulled
5 tablespoons wheat germ
3 tablespoons blackstrap molasses

Pour the yogurt and orange juice into a food processor and blend until smooth. Add the banana and strawberries. Process for ten seconds. Add the wheat germ and blackstrap molasses. Blend until all the ingredients are well mixed. Makes 2 glasses.

OTHER FRUIT DRINKS

GINGER TIME

This snappy soda is a good substitution for for an early evening alcoholic beverage.

1/4 cup ginger juice
1/4 cup cherry juice
2 teaspoons lime juice
2 tablespoons sugar
6 ice cubes, crushed
1 1/2 cups cold seltzer
2 lime slices

Put the ginger juice, cherry juice, lime juice and sugar in a small pitcher. Stir until the sugar is dissolved. Halve the crushed ice and fill the bottoms of two tall glasses. Pour the combined juice into the glasses. Add the seltzer and stir a few times. Garnish with the lime slices. Makes 2 large glasses.

MULLED SUNSHINE

For those cold winter days when you desire a reminder of warmer times.

3 cups pineapple juice
1 cup orange juice
1 cinnamon stick
4 whole cloves
2 tablespoons honey

Put the pineapple juice, orange juice, cinnamon stick, cloves and honey in a medium saucepan. Bring to a boil and then reduce the heat. Cover and simmer for 20 minutes. Remove the cinnamon and cloves. Serve hot in mugs. Serves 4.

SOUTHERN BERRY SODA

If peach fuzz had a taste it would taste like this soda.

1 cup raspberry juice
1 cup peach juice
2 tablespoons honey
1 1/2 cups seltzer
6 ice cubes, crushed

Combine the raspberry juice, peach juice and honey in medium pitcher. Stir until the honey is dissolved. Add the seltzer and stir twice. Halve the crushed ice and fill the bottoms of two tall glasses. Pour the juice-seltzer mix into both glasses and serve. Makes 2 large glasses.

CHERRY MINT–LIME RICKEY

This is a minty twist on the old cherry-lime rickey.

1/4 cup lime juice
2 tablespoons lemon juice
1/4 cup cherry juice
3 tablespoons fresh mint leaves, washed and coarsely chopped
2 tablespoons sugar
1 cup seltzer
3 ice cubes

Pour the lime juice, lemon juice and cherry juice into a blender or a food processor. Add the mint leaves and sugar. Blend until the mint has been puréed. Pour the mixture into a large glass and add the seltzer. Stir once. Add the ice cubes and enjoy. Makes 1 tall glass.

GREEN APPLE COOLER

A zippy, refreshing soda that matches an apple's tartness without the stomach upset.

1 cup apple juice
1/4 cup ginger juice
2 tablespoons lime juice
1 tablespoon sugar
1 1/4 cups cold seltzer
6 ice cubes

Pour the fruit juices into a medium pitcher. Add
the sugar and stir until the sugar is dissolved.
Add the seltzer and give the mixture two quick
stirs. Pour into two tall glasses and add three ice
cubes in each glass. Makes 2 servings.

MELON VERDE

Once a rare and exotic fruit, the kiwi is now
found in every supermarket.

1 cup kiwi fruit, peeled and sliced
1 cup white grape juice
1 cup honeydew melon juice
6 ice cubes, coarsely crushed
1/2 cup seltzer

Combine the kiwi fruit, grape juice and melon
juice in a food processor or blender. Process until
the kiwi is broken up. Add the crushed ice and
process until the mixture is smooth. Pour the
beverage into two tall glasses. Pour 1/4 cup of
seltzer into both glasses and stir twice. Makes 2
servings.

SOUPS

COLD TOMATO-YOGURT SOUP

A great cold soup for an outdoor dinner starter. For the best results use recently or just picked vine ripened tomatoes.

1 pound fresh tomatoes
1 scallion
1/2 cup yogurt
1 tablespoon dried chervil or 2 tablespoons fresh chopped chervil
salt and pepper to taste
several sprigs of fresh parsley

Wash the tomatoes in hot water to remove any wax. Trim the cores and cut into chunks small enough to fit your juicer. Juice the tomatoes and scallion. Add the juice to a blender. Add the yogurt, chervil, salt and pepper. Blend the ingredients until well mixed. Pour into serving bowls and decorate with one or two sprigs of parsley. Serves 2.

COLD HONEYDEW–PEAR SOUP

A soup which is fine as an appetizer or a light dessert.

1 large honeydew melon
3 ripe pears
2 tablespoons fresh lemon juice
1/2 cup dry white wine
1/8 teaspoon cinnamon
4 sprigs of fresh mint

Cut the melon in half. Remove the seeds and cut the melon from the rind. Slice the melon into juicer sized pieces and juice. Pour the melon juice into a large mixing bowl.

Peel and core the pears. Chop into small pieces and heat in a small heavy saucepan. Add the lemon juice. When the pears boil, reduce heat and cook for 10-12 minutes, stirring often, until soft. Pour into a food processor or blender and purée. Add the melon juice and blend. Add the wine and cinnamon and blend quickly. Pour the liquid into a serving bowl and chill. Garnish with several mint sprigs. Serves 4.

CUCUMBER–YOGURT SOUP

A light, satisfying soup for the hottest of summer days.

2 8-ounce containers plain low-fat yogurt
1/2 cup cucumber juice
1/2 cup cucumber pulp
1 teaspoon chopped garlic
1 teaspoon chopped fresh mint
1/2 teaspoon freshly ground black pepper

Empty the yogurt into a large bowl. Stir in the cucumber juice, pulp, garlic and mint. Let stand, covered, in the refrigerator for one hour. Serve in individual cups or bowls, sprinkled with pepper. Serves 4.

CARROT–TOMATO SOUP

Its quick and easy and a perfect way to begin a meaty meal.

1 cup tomato juice
1 cup carrot juice
1/2 cup chicken stock
2 teaspoons butter
1 tablespoon fresh parsley, chopped
2 teaspoons scallion, chopped, green part only

Combine the ingredients in a saucepan. Bring to a boil, stirring occasionally. Reduce the heat and simmer for 2 minutes. Serve hot. Makes 2 portions.

GINGER–CARROT JUICE SOUP

2 tablespoons vegetable oil
2 tablespoons butter
3 medium onions, chopped
2 cloves garlic, minced
3 cups carrot juice
1 1–inch cube fresh ginger, minced
1 tablespoon soy sauce
3 cups chicken stock
salt and pepper to taste

Heat the oil and melt the butter in a skillet. Add the onions and garlic. Saute until the onions are transparent. Add the carrot juice and simmer for 30 minutes. Add the ginger and soy sauce and simmer for 20 minutes. Transfer the soup to a food processor or blender and process until the mixture is smooth. Add the chicken stock and salt and pepper and blend. Pour the mixture into the skillet and heat until soup begins to bubble. Serves 8.

COLD RASPBERRY–RHUBARB SOUP

Late evening dinners will have a perfect beginning with this light soup.

2 cups rhubarb, coarsely chopped
1 cup fresh apple juice
1 tablespoon fresh lemon juice
1 cup fresh raspberries
8 tablespoons yogurt

Put the rhubarb and apple juice in a large saucepan. Cover and cook on a low flame for 45 minutes, stirring occasionally. Turn the heat off and allow to cool for 5 minutes. Put the rhubarb-apple mixture in a food processor or blender. Add the raspberries and lemon juice and purée. Pour the soup into a bowl and chill. Serve in individual bowls, garnished with two tablespoons of yogurt in the middle. Serves 4.

COLD BORSCHT

Cold borscht is an excellent way to introduce a non-juicer to the joys of juicing.

3 beets, quartered, with tops removed
1 cup fresh spinach
1/2 lemon
1 clove garlic
1 hard boiled egg, chopped
1 scallion, green part only, minced

Juice the beets, spinach, lemon and garlic. Pour mixture into two bowls. Sprinkle the chopped egg and scallion greens on the borscht. Chill for 30 minutes. Serves 2.

Variation: Substitute 1/2 cup yogurt for the hard boiled egg. Swirl the yogurt into the borscht.

CREAMY ASPARAGUS SOUP

On cold spring evenings this makes a delightful soup and tasty way begin dinner.

3 cups asparagus juice
1/2 cup asparagus pulp
3 eggs, beaten
2 cups half-and-half
2 teaspoons salt
1 tablespoon lemon juice

In a large saucepan, combine the asparagus juice and pulp. Bring the mixture to a boil. Reduce the heat and simmer for two minutes. Using a whisk or a fork slowly beat the eggs into the soup. Continue simmering the soup until the eggs are hard. Stir in the half-and-half, salt and lemon juice. Remove from heat and serve immediately. Makes 4 portions.

MAIN COURSES

ORANGE–CARROT POACHED TROUT

Whether it is store bought or freshly caught, this juiced recipe puts new life into the ordinary trout.

2 cups orange juice
1 cup carrot juice
1 cup water
3 tablespoons red wine vinegar
1 medium sized onion, sliced
1 teaspoon salt
8 whole peppercorns
2 whole allspice
1 bay leaf
4 parsley sprigs
2 large trout, about 2 pounds each
3 tablespoons butter
1/4 cup shallots, minced
3 tablespoons parsley, chopped
1/2 teaspoon tarragon, dried
salt and pepper to taste
2 tablespoons flour

Bring the orange juice, carrot juice, water, vinegar and onion to a boil in a large skillet. Add the salt. Tie the peppercorns, allspice, bay leaf and parsley in small cheesecloth square and make into a bag. Add the spice bouquet to the skillet and bring to a boil. Lower the heat and simmer for 30 minutes. Add the trout, cover and simmer for about 8 minutes or until the fish begins to flake. Remove the trout and place on a serving platter and keep warm. Remove the spice bouquet from the trout broth and reserve the liquid.

Melt the butter in a small saucepan. Add the shallots, parsley, tarragon, salt and pepper. Stirring constantly, cook the sauce until the shallots are tender. Stir in the flour and cook for two more minutes. Raise the heat to medium-high and slowly blend the trout broth into the sauce. Cook the mixture until it begins to boil. Reduce the heat and continue to cook until the sauce thickens. Pour over the trout and serve. 4 servings.

INDIAN PEPPER CHICKEN IS A SPICY, LOW-FAT MAIN COURSE

COD FISH STEW

3 tablespoons olive oil
1 onion, chopped
2 cloves garlic
1 cup cucumber juice
1/2 cup white wine
1 tablespoon soy sauce
1/2 teaspoon salt
1 teaspoon dried basil, crushed
or
1 tablespoon fresh basil, minced
1 bay leaf
2 cups potatoes, cubed
3/4 cup carrots, diced
1 pound fresh or frozen cod fish
1 1/2 cup tomatoes, chopped
1/2 cup mushrooms, sliced
2 tablespoons fresh parsley, chopped
1/4 cup water
2 tablespoons cornstarch
pepper to taste

Heat the olive oil in large saucepan. Add the chopped onion and garlic. Saute until the chopped onion is transparent. Stir in the cucumber juice, white wine, soy sauce, salt, basil, bay leaf, potatoes, mushrooms, carrots and pepper. Bring to a boil and cover. Reduce the heat. Simmer for 15-20 minutes, or until the vegetables soften. Add the fish, tomatoes and parsley. Cover and simmer until the fish flakes easily with a fork, about five minutes. Remove the fish and vegetables and place on a serving plate. In a bowl, mix the water and cornstarch. Stir the cornstarch mixture into sauce in the saucepan. Cook until the sauce thickens. Pour the sauce over the fish and vegetables. Makes 4 portions.

INDIAN PEPPER CHICKEN

A hearty low-fat entree that rivals the best Indian restaurant fare.

1 2-3 pound chicken
1 piece of fresh ginger, 1-inch cube, peeled and roughly chopped
5 cloves garlic, chopped
1 large onion, roughly chopped
1/4 cup slivered almonds
1 quart (4 cups) sweet red pepper juice
3 tablespoons Indian curry powder
2 teaspoons ground cumin
cayenne to taste
2 teaspoons salt
1/2 cup vegetable oil
1 cup water
1/4 cup lemon juice

Skin and quarter the chicken. Separate the wings from the breast, quarter the breast and detach the thighs from the legs. Put the garlic, onion and almonds in a food processor and process until the onions are well minced. Add the sweet red pepper juice, Indian curry powder, ground cumin, cayenne pepper, ginger and salt. Blend until well mixed with the red pepper juice.

Pour the oil into a heavy casserole on top of the stove. Heat the oil on a medium high flame. Add the red pepper mixture and stirring often, fry for about 10 minutes. Preheat the oven to 375. Stir in the water and lemon juice. Add the chicken. Remove from heat and cover. Place the casserole in the oven. Bake at 375 for 10 minutes, reduce the heat to 350, stir a few times and bake for 20 minutes. Uncover the casserole and cook for 10 more minutes. Remove casserole and serve with rice. Serves 4

SOLE WITH CUCUMBER FOOL

A fool is an old English dessert made from stewed, puréed fruit and heavy cream. This fish dish is both light and not sweet, using egg whites instead of cream and cucumber in place of fruit, and a perfect dinner entree for warm weather.

4 fillets of sole
white wine
4 egg whites
1/2 cup cucumber juice
2 shallots finely chopped
2 tablespoons mild, white wine vinegar
2 tablespoons cucumber, peeled, seeded and
    finely chopped
2 tablespoons heavy cream

Fold the fillets in half and gently poach in half water, half dry white wine to cover. In the meantime, beat the egg whites to light peaks. Boil the shallots and vinegar until reduced almost to an emulsion. Fold the juice, cucumber and shallot mixture gently into the egg whites, along with the heavy cream. Remove the fillets to an ovenproof dish. Top each with a few spoonfuls of the egg white mixture, smoothing it out to completely cover the fish. Put under the broiler just until the tops are lightly browned and serve immediately. Serves 4.

SHRIMP IN BASIL–TOMATO BROTH

2 pounds large shrimp, shelled and deveined
1 shallot
1 pound ripe tomatoes, cored
1/2 cup basil leaves, finely chopped
1 tablespoon lemon juice

Juice the shallot and tomatoes together. In the resulting juice, poach the shrimp for five minutes over medium heat. Add the lemon juice and basil and cook one minute longer. Serve immediately with rice or pasta. Serves 4.

ROAST PORK WITH PEACH JUICE

Modern breeding methods have made pork almost as lean as chicken and appreciably lower in fat and cholesterol than beef, lamb or veal. Try this roast for a grand dinner party.

1 3-pound boneless loin of pork, rolled and tied
2 cloves garlic, slivered
1 cup peach juice
1 teaspoon ground coriander
1 teaspoon ground ginger

Make a number of deep incisions in the pork with a sharp knife, inserting slivers of garlic in each. Place the pork in a roasting pan, fat side up in a 350 degree oven. Roast for a total of one and one-half hours, turning the heat up to 400 degrees for the last 15 minutes. During the roasting baste with the peach juice combined with the ginger and coriander. The essence of peaches will permeate the meat and a lovely glaze will result. Let the roast stand in a serving platter for 15 minutes before carving. Serve with broccoli, small new potatoes in their skins and a sweet-and-sour chutney or relish in lieu of gravy. Serves 4-6 depending on how substantial other parts of the meal are.

PASTA WITH TUNA SAUCE

An unusual combination, typical of the Ligurian coast of Northern Italy. It makes a fast, delicious meal, accompanied by a salad and dry white wine.

2 cloves garlic, chopped
1 7-ounce can tuna in olive oil
pulp from tomatoes
1 cup tomato juice made from Italian plum
  tomatoes
1/2 cup fresh basil leaves, finely chopped
1 teaspoon capers, roughly chopped
1 pound short, tubular pasta—ziti, penne, etc.

First, make the sauce. Sauté garlic in the oil drained from the tuna. Add the tomato pulp and cook for two minutes over medium heat. Add the remaining ingredients, except the pasta and continue cooking for 10 minutes until well-blended and slightly reduced. Cook the pasta in plenty of boiling, salted water until al dente, slightly resistant to the tooth. Drain pasta and immediately place in a heated, large bowl, add the sauce and toss thoroughly. Serve immediately. Serves 4.

CITRUS BARBECUE CHICKEN

A fresh alternative to the same old barbecue sauce.

1 chicken, cut into moderate sized pieces
3/4 cup lemon juice
1 large onion, cut into eighths
4 cloves garlic
1/2 cup vegetable oil
1 1/2 cups orange juice
1/4 cup soy sauce
2 tablespoons honey
2 tablespoons Dijon mustard

Put the lemon juice, onion, and garlic in a food processor. Process the mixture for 15 seconds. Pour in the vegetable oil and orange juice. Process again for 15 seconds. Add the soy sauce, honey and Dijon mustard. Process for last time until the liquid is smoothly textured.

Put the chicken pieces into a plastic bag. Pour in the marinade making sure that all of the chicken is covered. Squeeze the air out the plastic bag and seal. Marinade the chicken for a least a half and hour, but no more than 90 minutes. Remove the chicken from the plastic bag and place on a hot barbecue. Turn the chicken after 20 minutes and brush with the remaining marinade. Cook for 20 more minutes or until done. Serves 4-6

VEGETARIAN PILAF

1/4 cup vegetable oil (olive preferred)
1 onion, chopped
1 carrot, chopped
1 red pepper, peeled, seeded and chopped
1 clove garlic, chopped
1/2 cup almonds or pecans, coarsely chopped
2 cups long-grain rice
1/4 cup celery juice
2 tablespoons lemon juice

In the oil, sauté the onion, carrot, pepper, garlic and nuts, until the pepper is limp and all are lightly browned. Add the rice and let it take on color for two or three minutes. Add enough water to cover the rice by one finger. Cover the pot and simmer, stirring occasionally, until the liquid is absorbed. This will depend on the quality and age of the rice. Add the juices, cover and let stand for five minutes off the heat. Serves 4-6.

MARINADES AND SAUCES

GREEN FISH SAUCE

A quick and easy way to add a little extra to firm fleshed fish.

5 tablespoons olive oil
1 medium onion, chopped
1 garlic clove, finely chopped
2 cups string bean juice
1 tablespoon lemon juice
1/2 teaspoon salt
1/4-1/2 teaspoon freshly ground black pepper, to taste

Heat the olive oil in a medium skillet. Add the onion and garlic. Sauté until the onion is transparent. Pour the string bean juice into the skillet and bring to a boil. Reduce the heat and simmer uncovered for five minutes. Stir in the lemon juice, salt and pepper. Makes 2 cups.

GINGER–LIME–CARROT MARINADE

For best results use this marinade on chicken or pork. The recipe is easily doubled.

1 1/2 cups carrot juice
1/2 cup lime juice
1 tablespoon salt
3 tablespoons vegetable oil
2 tablespoons honey
1 1-inch square of lime peel, coarsely chopped
1 1-inch cube of ginger root, coarsely chopped

Combine all the ingredients in a food processor or blender. Process until the ginger root almost disappears. Put the chicken, cut into eighths, into a large plastic bag. Add the marinade and squeeze out all the air. Seal the bag. Move the chicken in the sealed bag so that every piece is in contact with the marinade. Marinate at least 30 minutes, but no more than an hour. Follow your favorite broiling or barbecue procedure. Makes 2 1/4 cups.

ORANGE–BEET MARINADE

This marinade is an easy way to perk-up your favorite meat stew. It works especially well with pork or lamb.

1/2 cup beet juice
1 cup orange juice
3 tablespoons red wine vinegar
1/2 onion, coarsely chopped
3 tablespoons brown sugar
1 teaspoon salt

Combine the ingredients in food processor or blender. Process until the onions are finely minced. Put the meat, cut into 1-inch cubes, into a large plastic bag. Add the marinade and squeeze out all the air. Seal the bag. Move the meat in the sealed bag so that every piece is in contact with the marinade. Marinate at least 30 minutes, but no more than an hour. Follow your favorite stew recipe. Makes 2 1/4 cups.

RED WINE-PEAR MARINADE

1/2 bottle dry red wine
1 large onion, chopped
1 cup pear juice
1 large sprig fresh tarragon

Combine all ingredients in a large glass, enameled or stainless steel bowl. Use as a marinade for lamb or veal. Let meat marinate for at least two hours. Pat dry and grill or roast.

RED PEPPER–CURRY SAUCE

2 tablespoons vegetable oil
3 tablespoons vegetable pulp
    (pepper and carrot preferred)
1 medium onion, finely chopped
1 clove garlic, minced
2 tablespoons red wine vinegar
2 cups red pepper juice
2 teaspoons curry powder
1 tablespoon lemon juice
salt to taste

Heat the oil in a saucepan. Add the vegetable pulp, onion and garlic. Sauté until the onion is transparent. Stir in the vinegar and cook, on medium heat, for a minute. Add the pepper juice and cook for three minutes. Add the curry powder, lemon juice and salt. Cook, stirring, for five minutes. Makes 3 cups.

MARINARA SAUCE

When using this recipe, remember only vegetable pulp should be employed. Pulp containing carrots, celery and leafy greens is the best.

7 tablespoons olive oil, extra virgin preferred
1 large onion, chopped
4 cloves garlic, minced
1 cup vegetable pulp
1 28-ounce can of imported Italian tomatoes, or 2 pounds fresh vine-ripened tomatoes, cores removed, chopped
1 teaspoon dried basil
1 teaspoon dried marjoram
1/2 teaspoon dried thyme
2 tablespoons capers
salt and pepper to taste

Heat the olive oil in a large saucepan. Add the chopped onion and garlic. Sauté on medium high heat until the chopped onion is soft. Add the pulp and sauté for two minutes. Cut up the canned tomatoes and add whatever sauce is in the can. Reduce the heat to medium and stir in the basil, marjoram and thyme. Partially cover and cook for 5 minutes. Add the capers and cook for another 20 minutes partially covered on a medium low flame. Add salt and pepper to taste.

If using fresh tomatoes, follow the instructions as for canned tomatoes except: cook for10 minutes before adding the capers. Serves 4-6.

FISH STEAK MARINADE

Tuna and swordfish go well with this all-purpose marinade.

1/4 cup lemon juice
1/4 cup lime juice
1 teaspoon dried tarragon, crushed
or
1 tablespoon fresh tarragon, minced
1 teaspoon Dijon mustard
1 clove garlic, chopped
1/4 cup olive oil

Blend all the ingredients in a food processor or blender until well mixed. Pour the marinade into a shallow baking pan, large enough to hold the fish steak. Put the fish steak in the shallow baking pan and let marinate in the refrigerator for 30 minutes a side.

A SELECTION OF JUICE MARINADES

DIPS AND DRESSINGS

BROCCOLI DIP

1/2 cup broccoli juice
1/2 cup (4 ounces) cream cheese, softened
1/2 cup (4 ounces) sharp cheddar cheese, grated
2 cloves garlic, chopped
2 tablespoons Worcestershire sauce
1/4 cup broccoli flowers, chopped
1/8 teaspoon salt

Put the broccoli juice and cream cheese in a food processor or blender. Process until smooth. Add the cheddar cheese, garlic and Worcestershire sauce. Process again until the cheddar cheese is well distributed throughout the dip. Add the broccoli and salt and blend. Makes 2 cups.

SUMMER DIP

1 7-ounce package cream cheese
1/2 cup cucumber pulp
4 radishes, finely chopped
2 tablespoons onion, finely chopped
lemon juice to taste
freshly ground black pepper to taste

Mash cream cheese, thinning with lemon juice. Add the remaining ingredients and whip until smooth. If the dip is too thick, thin with yogurt or milk to desired consistency.

PEACH–PEAR DRESSING

Ideal for fruit salads. It is also good as pastry and poached fruit topping.

1 cup peach juice
1 pear, seeded and cored
1 tablespoon lemon juice
1 tablespoon honey
1/8 teaspoon cinnamon

Combine all the ingredients in a food processor. Process until smooth. Transfer the mixture to a saucepan. Cook under low heat until the dressing begins to thicken. Remove and let cool. Makes 1 3/4 cups.

ASIAN CARROT DRESSING

Not only is the Asian carrot dressing good with green salads, it can be used on steamed vegetables as well. This dressing gets better with age. You can store it in a jar, with tight fitting lid, for up to one week.

3 tablespoons soy sauce
1/4 cup carrot juice
1 scallion, coarsely chopped
1 clove garlic, coarsely chopped
1 1/2-inch cube ginger root, coarsely chopped
1 cup peanut oil, vegetable oil may be substituted
6 teaspoons rice wine vinegar

Put the soy sauce and carrot juice in a blender or food processor. Process until well mixed. Add the scallion, garlic and ginger root. Process again until the solid ingredients are minced. Slowly add half the oil while the processor or blender is still running. Add the vinegar and the remaining oil. Blend again. Makes 2 cups.

LEMON DRESSING

This tart dressing is good on steamed vegetables.

1 teaspoon water
1/4 teaspoon salt, or to taste
1/8 teaspoon lemon peel, grated
2 teaspoons dried mint
4 tablespoons lemon juice
1/2 cup olive oil
1/2 teaspoon black pepper

Combine the water, salt and lemon peel in a jar with a tight fitting lid. Let stand for two minutes. Add the mint and lemon juice, cover and shake. Add the olive oil and black pepper. Cover and shake once more. Serve immediately. Makes 1 cup.

APPLE–BASIL DRESSING

1/2 cup olive oil
1/4 cup apple juice
1 tablespoon fresh basil leaves, chopped
1 tablespoon lemon juice
1/4 teaspoon freshly ground black pepper
1 clove chopped garlic (optional)

Combine all ingredients in a screw-cap jar and shake vigorously until well blended. Let sit for at least one hour to give flavors time to meld and develop. Shake again before dressing salad.

ZESTY ITALIAN DRESSING

For the best results do not economize—use extra virgin olive oil and balsamic vinegar where called for. This dressing can be stored in the refrigerator for several days.

1 cup celery juice
1 teaspoon dried basil
1/4 teaspoon dried oregano
1/4 teaspoon dried thyme
1/4 teaspoon salt
1 clove garlic, roughly chopped
1 scallion, roughly chopped
1 cup extra virgin olive oil
3 tablespoons balsamic vinegar
2 tablespoons red wine vinegar
1/4 cup regular olive oil

Put the celery juice, basil, oregano, thyme, salt, garlic and scallion in a food processor. Blend until the garlic and scallion are in small pieces. Add half the extra virgin olive oil and process once more for 5 seconds. Pour the remaining extra virgin olive oil into the food processor along with the balsamic vinegar and red wine vinegar. Process until garlic and scallion are minced. Run the food processor again, slowly adding the olive oil. Keep processing for 10 seconds. The last addition of olive oil should thicken the dressing a bit. Makes 2 1/2 cups of dressing.

HERB DRESSING

A great way to enjoy the summer when the lettuce is fresh and your herbs can be picked from the garden. If you plan to use fresh herbs multiply the recipe amount by three.

1/2 cup celery juice
1/2 teaspoon dried chives
1/2 teaspoon dried chervil
1/2 teaspoon dried summer savory
1/2 teaspoon dried basil
1/4 teaspoon salt
1/4 teaspoon freshly ground black pepper
1 scallion, coarsely chopped
1 clove garlic, coarsely chopped
2 sprigs of parsley, coarsely chopped
1 cup extra virgin or regular olive oil
3-4 tablespoons of tarragon vinegar, to taste

Put all the ingredients except the olive oil and vinegar in a food processor. Process until the scallion and garlic are minced. Add half the olive oil and blend. Pour the remaining olive oil and vinegar into the food processor and process until the dressing is well mixed. Makes 2 cups.

SORBETS

Almost any of the single, double or fun drinks can be made into a sorbet. The secret is in the freezing. After making the juice, pour the mixture into a ice cube freezer tray. Freeze until almost solid. Remove the cubes and put into a food processor or blender. At this point one or more liquid ingredients may be added. *The one important ingredient that must be added at this stage is one egg white.* Process until the cubes have become a thick slush. Return the mixture to the freezer and freeze until the desired texture, soft or firm, is obtained.

PEAR–AMARETTO SORBET

A sweet yet delicate sorbet for an evening by the fireplace.

2 1/2 cups pear juice
3 tablespoons sugar
1/2 cup water
2 tablespoons lime juice
1 egg white
3 tablespoons Amaretto

Put the pear juice, sugar, water and lime juice in a large jar with a tight fitting lid. Shake or stir until the sugar is dissolved. Pour into a freezer ice cube tray. Freeze until almost solid. Remove the cubes and put into a food processor or blender. Add the egg white and Amaretto. Process until the cubes have become a thick slush. Pour the sorbet into a bowl and return the mixture to the freezer. Freeze until the desired texture, soft or firm, is obtained. Makes 6 servings.

MELON–GO–ROUND

A perfect summer treat, when the melons are ripe and the living is easy.

1 cup watermelon juice
1 cup honeydew juice
5 strawberries, hulled and frozen
1/4 cup honey
1/4 teaspoon nutmeg
1 egg white

Combine the watermelon juice, honeydew juice, strawberries, honey and nutmeg in a food processor or blender. Process until the strawberries are minced. Pour the mixture into an ice cube tray. Freeze. Remove the cubes and put into a food processor or blender. Add the egg white and process until the mixture is soft. Pour the sorbet into a bowl and return the mixture to the freezer. Freeze until the sorbet is firm. Makes 6 servings.

TANGY GRAPE

Not your ordinary grape sorbet. The tartness of this dessert makes it a perfect end to a rich dinner.

1 1/4 cups green seedless grape juice
1/4 cup lime juice
1/2 cup water
3 tablespoons sugar
1 egg white

Put the grape juice, lime juice, water and sugar in a large jar with a tight fitting lid. Shake or stir until the sugar is dissolved. Pour into an ice cube tray. Freeze. Remove the cubes from the tray and put into a food processor or blender. Add the egg white and process until the mixture becomes slushy. Pour the sorbet into a bowl and return the mixture to the freezer. The sorbet is ready when the mixture has frozen to a firm texture. Makes 6 portions.

APPLE–BLUEBERRY CREAM

When is a pie not a pie—when it is an apple-blueberry cream sorbet.

1 1/4 cups apple juice
1 cup blueberries
1/2 cup water
1/2 teaspoon cinnamon, ground
3 tablespoons honey
3 tablespoons heavy cream

Combine the apple juice, blueberries, water and cinnamon in a food processor or blender. Process until the blueberries are minced. Pour the mixture into an ice cube tray. Freeze. Remove the cubes and put into a food processor or blender. Add the honey and cream. Blend until the mixture is thick. Pour the sorbet into a bowl and return the mixture to the freezer. Freeze until the sorbet is firm. Serves 6.

RASPBERRY COOLER

The ideal accompaniment for a lawn picnic.

1 1/2 cups white wine
1 cup raspberries, washed
2 tablespoons sugar
1/4 cup water
1 tablespoon brandy

Combine the wine and raspberries in a food processor or blender. Process until the raspberries are minced. Add the sugar, water and brandy. Process again and pour the liquid into an ice cube tray. Freeze until the cubes are almost hard. Remove the cubes and put into a food processor or blender. Blend until the mixture is thick. Pour the sorbet into a bowl and return the mixture to the freezer. Freeze until the desired texture, soft or firm, is obtained. Serves 6.

APPLE–PLUM SORBET

This sorbet makes a great autumn dessert.

1 cup apple juice
2 cups plums, halved and pitted
3 tablespoons sugar
1/8 teaspoon allspice
1/2 cup water
1 tablespoon lemon juice
1 egg white

Combine all ingredients except the egg white in a food processor or blender. Process until the plums have pulverized. Pour into a ice cube tray. Freeze. Remove the cubes from the tray and put into a food processor or blender. Add the egg white and process until the mixture becomes slushy. Pour the sorbet into a bowl and return to the freezer. The sorbet is ready when the mixture has frozen to a firm texture. Makes 6 portions.

MANGO–PEAR SORBET

Bright and tasty treat that kids from nine to ninety will adore.

2 cups mangoes, peeled, seeded and cubed
1 1/4 cups pear juice
1/2 cup water
3 tablespoons sugar
1 tablespoon lime juice
1/4 cup heavy cream

In a food processor or blender, put the mangoes, pear juice, water, sugar and lime juice. Process until smooth. Pour the mixture in an ice cube tray. Freeze and remove before the cubes are solid. Put the cubes back into the food processor or blender with the cream. Blend until the mixture is thick. Pour the sorbet into a bowl and freeze until firm. Serves 6.

TOMATO ICE

1 1/2 cups tomato juice
2 tablespoons scallion juice
2 tablespoons lemon juice
2 tablespoons tomato pulp
1/2 cup water
1 clove garlic
3 tablespoons fresh basil, chopped
2 tablespoons soy sauce
1/4 teaspoon cayenne or to taste

FRESH JUICE SORBETS ARE A FITTING END TO ANY MEAL

Combine all the ingredients in a food processor
or blender. Process until the garlic is minced.
Pour the mixture into an ice cube tray and freeze.
Remove before the cubes have become solid. Put
into a food processor and blend until the mixture
becomes slushy. Pour the sorbet into a bowl and
freeze. Makes 6 portions.

CUCUMBER FRAPPÉ

A refreshing sorbet to be served instead of a cold
soup.

1 1/2 cups cucumber juice
1/4 cup fresh parsley, coarsely chopped
2 tablespoons fresh mint, coarsely chopped
1 scallion, coarsely chopped
1/4 cup water
salt and pepper, to taste
1 cup yogurt

In a food processor or blender, combine all the
ingredients except the yogurt. Process until the
scallion is minced. Pour into an ice cube tray and
freeze until almost solid. Remove the ice cubes.
Put the ice cubes in a food processor and process
until soft but not watery. Add the yogurt and
process once more until well mixed. Pour mixture into a bowl and freeze until firm. Serves 6.

BAKING AND DESSERTS

VERY ORANGE COOKIES

1/3 cup butter
1/3 cup shortening
1 cup honey
1 egg, white and yolk
1 tablespoon lemon peel, grated
2/3 cup orange pulp
2 1/4 cups flour
1 teaspoon baking powder
1/2 teaspoon baking soda
1/2 teaspoon salt
1/2 cup fresh orange juice

In a mixing bowl, cream the butter and shortening for a minute . Keep creaming and slowly add small amounts of the honey to the mixture. Blend in the egg, lemon peel and orange pulp. Alternately add, in small batches, the dry ingredients and the orange juice. Continue to cream until the mixture is well-blended.

Chill the dough for half an hour. Preheat the oven to 375 degrees. Remove the dough from the refrigerator and drop teaspoon-sized portions of dough on a greased baking sheet. Place the baking sheet in the oven and bake at 375 degrees for 15 minutes or until the cookies are lightly brown.

APPLE GOODIES

2 cups sifted flour
1 teaspoon baking soda
1/2 cup butter
1 cup brown sugar, packed
1/2 teaspoon salt
1 teaspoon cinnamon
teaspoon ginger
1/2 teaspoon nutmeg
1 egg
1 cup chopped pecans
1 cup finely chopped unpared apple
1 cup mixed dark and light raisins, chopped
1/4 cup apple juice

Preheat oven to 400 degrees. Sift flour with baking soda. Mix butter, brown sugar , salt, cinnamon, ginger, nutmeg and egg until well blended. Stir in the flour mixture, then the nuts, apple and raisins. Blend in apple juice. Onto greased cookie sheets, drop rounded tablespoons of dough, 2 inches apart. Bake 10 to 15 minutes or until golden. Allow to rest on sheets briefly before removing to cooling racks. Cool completely.

ZUCCHINI–CARROT CAKE

CAKE
2 eggs
1 cup sugar
2/3 cup vegetable oil
1 1/4 cups flour
1 teaspoon baking powder
1 teaspoon baking soda
1 teaspoon cinnamon
1/2 teaspoon salt
1 cup carrot pulp
1 cup zucchini pulp
1 cup chopped nuts

FROSTING
3-ounce package cream cheese, softened
3 tablespoons butter
1 teaspoon vanilla extract
1 cup powdered sugar

Preheat over to 350 degrees. Beat eggs with sugar until frothy. Gradually beat in oil. Add dry ingredients. Beat at high speed for 4 minutes. Stir in carrot and zucchini pulps and nuts. Pour into 9-inch square baking pan. Bake for 35 minutes or until top springs back when lightly touched. For frosting: In a small bowl blend cream cheese, and butter, add sugar and vanilla. Beat until smooth. Spread evenly over cooled cake.

ZUCCHINI BREAD

3 eggs
1 1/2 cups sugar
1 cup vegetable oil
2 cups zucchini pulp
1/2 cup milk
3 teaspoons vanilla extract
3 cups all-purpose flour
1 teaspoon salt
1 teaspoon baking soda
1/4 teaspoon double-acting baking powder
3 teaspoons ground cinnamon
1 cup coarsely chopped walnuts or pecans

Preheat oven to 350 degrees. Beat the eggs until light and foamy. Add the sugar, oil, zucchini pulp and vanilla, and mix lightly but well. Combine flour, milk, salt, soda, baking powder and cinnamon and add to the egg-zucchini mixture. Stir until well blended, add nuts and pour into two 9x5x3-inch greased loaf pans. Bake for 1 hour or until cake tester comes out clean. Cool on racks.

LEMON LOAF—LIGHT AND MOIST

LEMON LOAF

1/2 cup butter
1/2 cup granulated sugar
Rind of one lemon, finely chopped or coarsely
grated
2 eggs
1/2 cup lemon juice
2 cups all-purpose flour
3 teaspoons double-acting baking powder
1 teaspoon salt

Preheat oven to 350 degrees. Cream the butter and sugar together, then add the lemon rind and the eggs one at a time, beating well after each is added. Stir in the lemon juice, then sift in dry ingredients gradually. Beat well after each addition until you have a light batter. Pour into a greased and floured 8 x4x2-inch pan and bake for 50 to 60 minutes or until a cake tester comes out clean. Cool in the pan for 10 minutes and then turn out on the rack. Allow to age one day before serving.

APPLE–NUT CAKE

1/3 cup butter
1 cup sugar
2 eggs
1 teaspoon vanilla extract
1 1/2 cups all-purpose flour
1 teaspoon baking powder
1 teaspoon baking soda
1 teaspoon salt
1 teaspoon cinnamon
1/2 teaspoon nutmeg
1/2 teaspoon ginger
2 cups apple pulp
1/2 cup apple juice
1/2 cup raisins
3/4 cups chopped walnuts or pecans

Preheat the oven to 350 degrees. Grease and flour an 8-inch square pan. In a large bowl , beat the butter until smooth and creamy. Gradually add the sugar and continue beating until well blended. Add the eggs and vanilla and beat well. Combine the flour, baking powder, baking soda, salt, cinnamon, nutmeg and ginger, and sift them together into the butter-sugar mixture. Beat until smooth and well blended; the mixture will be very stiff. Add the apple pulp, apple juice, raisins and nuts, beat well. Spread into the prepared pan. Bake for 30 to 35 minutes or until a cake tester comes out clean. Remove from the oven and cool on a rack. Cool before serving.

ORANGE–CARROT BREAD

6 tablespoons butter
1 cup sugar
1/4 cup honey
1/2 teaspoon cinnamon
1/4 teaspoon nutmeg
1 tablespoon coarsely grated orange peel
1 egg
1 1/4 cups carrot pulp
1/4 cup carrot juice
1/3 cup orange juice
1 1/2 cups all-purpose flour
1 teaspoon baking powder
1 teaspoon baking soda
1/8 teaspoon salt
3/4 cup chopped walnuts or hazelnuts

Preheat oven to 350 degrees. Cream the butter and sugar with a mixer, beating until thoroughly incorporated. Add the honey, cinnamon, nutmeg, orange peel, egg, carrot pulp and juice and orange juice. Thoroughly mix the dry ingredients and the nuts, then blend with the liquid mixture until all the flour is moistened. Turn the batter into a greased 9-inch loaf pan and bake for 1 hour. Let rest in the pan for 15 minutes before turning out on a rack to cool.

BAKED BANANAS

4 ripe bananas
1 stick sweet butter
1 pint ripe strawberries
2 limes
sugar or honey to taste

Peel bananas. Melt butter in a flat baking dish. Coat bananas with butter and arrange in dish. Bake 15-20 minutes at 350 degrees until hot through and browned. Juice the berries and limes. Combine the juice with one-half the resulting pulp and reduce in a saucepan by half. Add sweetening to taste. Pour over the baked fruit and serve either hot or cold. Serves 4

FRUIT SALAD WITH MANGO SAUCE

A selection fresh fruits appropriate to the sea
    son—bananas, peaches, apples, figs, plums,
    cherries, etc.—all cut into medium size
    chunks or slices
1 large mango, very ripe
sugar to taste
1 tablespoon kirsch per serving

Combine all the fruits except the mango in a large bowl. Juice the mango. Combine mango pulp with the juice, sugar to taste and the kirsch and whirl a few seconds in a blender. Pour over the fruits and let stand for one hour.

ABOUT THE AUTHOR

Lionel Murphy is a writer and photographer living in New York. He is the author of *Sensational Salads*, *Unknown Mysteries*, *Gold Rushes of North America* and *Murders in America*. His photography has appeared in many national publications and in galleries and collections around the world.